LIVIN ON RIVERS

Written by Nizrana Farook
Illustrated by Paul Boston

Contents

OXFORD
UNIVERSITY PRESS

Words to look out for ...

benefit *NOUN*
A benefit is something that is useful or helpful.

hint *NOUN*
a useful idea or piece of advice

monitor *VERB*
To monitor something is to watch it or test it regularly, in order to see what is happening.

responsible *ADJECTIVE*
To be responsible for something is to be the cause of it.

sample *NOUN*
A small amount that shows what something is like.

underneath
PREPOSITION
below or beneath

Rivers and us

All around the world, people live near, beside and even on rivers.

There are many benefits to living near a river. Over time, people have changed their lives so that they live close to them.

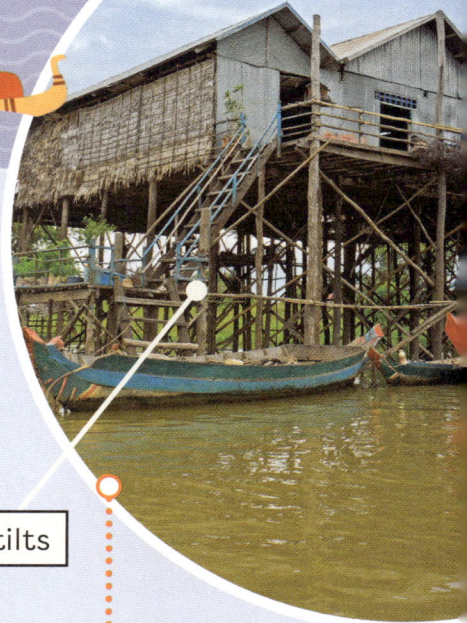

stilts

This house sits on stilts over a river.

This floating market has existed on a river for over a hundred years.

There are even river theatres!

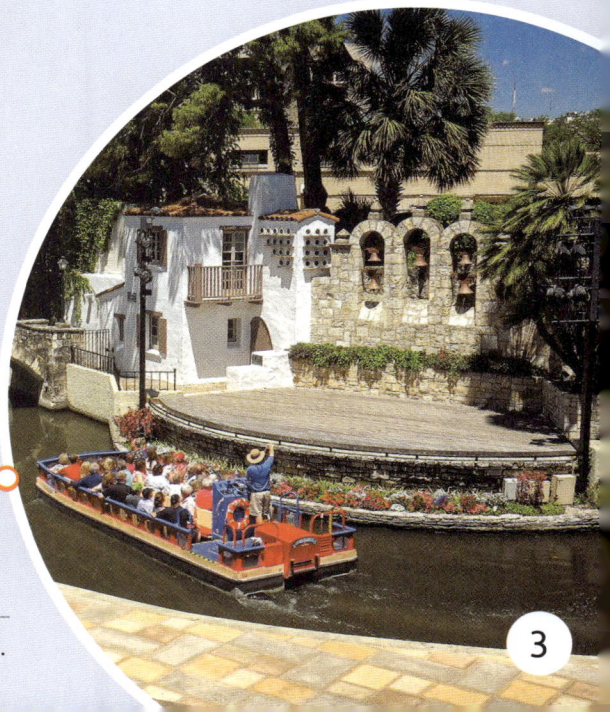

A benefit is something that is useful or helpful.

Early river civilizations

Some of the earliest **civilizations** appeared near large rivers.

More than 6000 years ago, people settled near two large rivers in Western Asia.

They could use the rivers to travel long distances.

The rivers gave the people everything they needed to live there.

Later, people settled by the Nile River in Egypt. The river gave the people a good source of water. It also protected them from enemies because it was hard to cross.

These people went on to become the ancient Egyptians.

This ancient Egyptian carving tells us about river life thousands of years ago.

Living by rivers

Imagine you were setting up home in the middle of nowhere. What is the most important thing you would need? Here's a hint: rivers contain a lot of it!

Water is necessary for life, so access to it would come high on your list. You would need water for drinking, washing and preparing food.

A hint is a useful idea or piece of advice.

You would need to grow food as well. The **fertile** soil near a river is perfect for growing things. A river would also give you a good supply of water for your farm.

The fish in the river would provide food. Other animals would also come to the river to drink water. This means that you would have a choice of food between fish and meat.

You could travel to other places by boat and take things with you to trade. Other people could bring things to you as well.

These are some of the reasons early humans chose to live next to rivers, too.

Rivers allowed early civilizations to grow and develop.

Travelling on rivers

The earliest form of river transport was a type of canoe.

A canoe is a small, narrow boat. Many **cultures** around the world used them for transport and hunting. They used to be carved out of tree trunks.

Today, canoeing can be a competitive sport or a fun activity.

This is the earliest known canoe. It is around 10 000 years old!

a modern canoe

Boats called kayaks were used by **Indigenous peoples** in the Arctic. They were used for hunting and exploring hard-to-reach places.

Kayaks were originally made from animal skins stretched over a frame made from wood or bone. They were covered in these skins to protect people's legs from icy water.

a model of an early kayak

Kayaking is now a popular hobby.

Rivers today

We still rely on rivers.

In many cities, tap water comes from the nearby river. To make the water safe to drink, dirt and germs have to be removed. **Chemicals** are added to clean the water. It is also put through special **filters**.

Water is sent to people's taps through pipes that run <u>underneath</u> the ground.

River water is cleaned in a treatment **plant**.

<u>Underneath</u> means below or beneath.

Rivers still provide a good way of getting around. Travelling by boat can make journeys quicker. Boats also create less pollution than cars and aeroplanes.

a passenger boat

Rivers help control flooding. When there is a lot of rain, the water drains into rivers. The extra water is carried away.

rainwater draining into a river

River power!

Rivers can be used to make electricity. This is called hydropower.

Water flows from a **dam** and turns a wheel (called a turbine) really fast. The energy from this movement is turned into electricity by a **generator**.

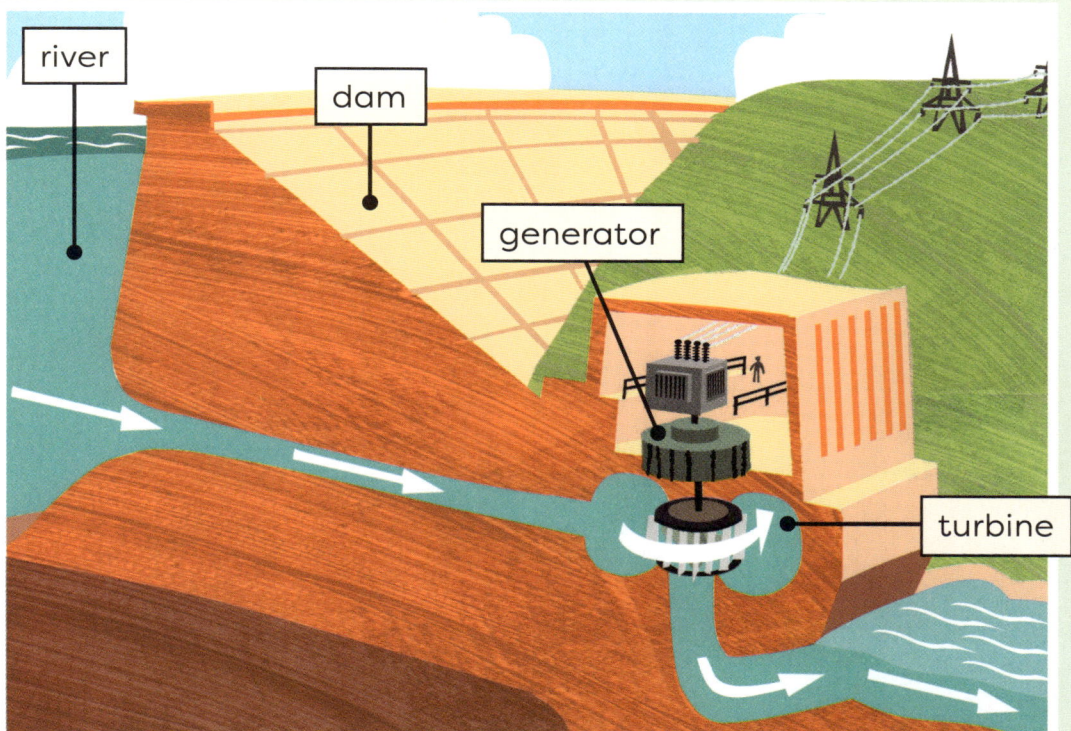

river

dam

generator

turbine

Hydropower doesn't create air pollution, which means it is better for the environment.

Kampong Ayer village

Hello! My name is Noraini. I live with my family in a special village on the Brunei River. Brunei is a country in South East Asia.

A long time ago, my village was part of an important trade route. However, the area around the river has always flooded. To get around this, our houses were built on stilts!

Brunei

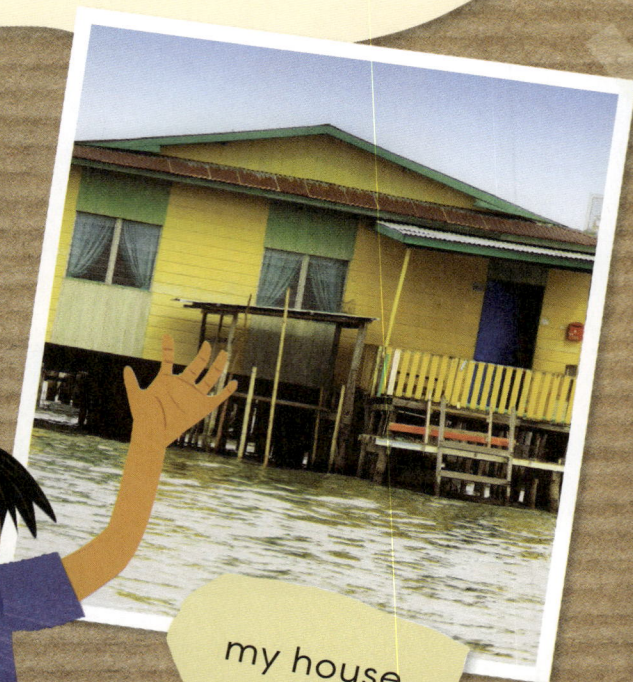

my house

My parents work in the fishing industry, just like my grandparents did. I go to school on land. To get there, I take a water taxi. I like school, but I'm always glad to get home.

I like to go exploring with my cousins in the afternoons, running along the walkways that connect all our houses.

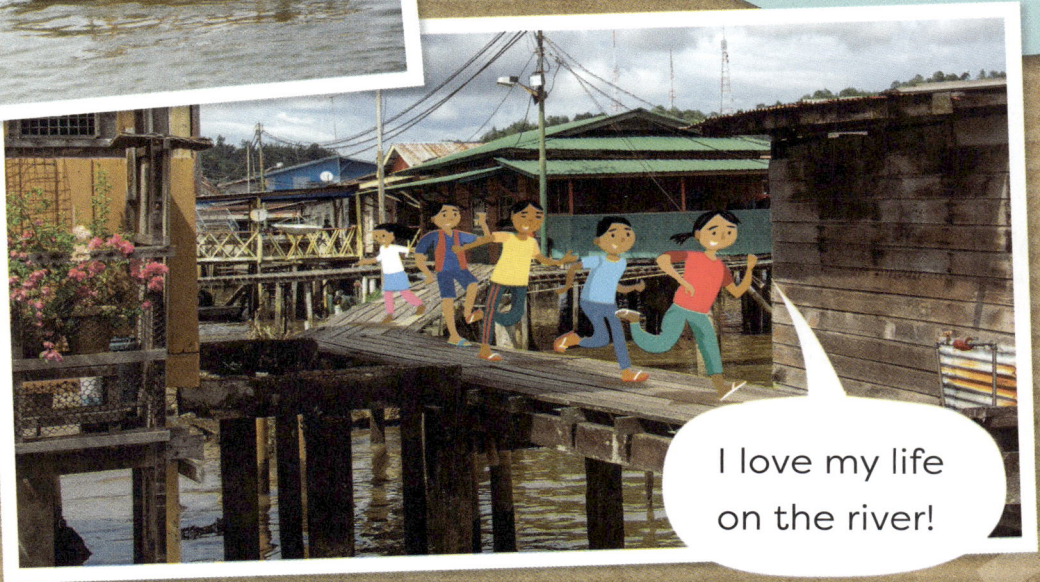

a water taxi

I love my life on the river!

Sacred rivers

Rivers have played a large part in people's beliefs for thousands of years.

In ancient Egypt, the flooding of the River Nile each year was seen as a gift from the god Hapi (say: *Ha-pee*). The flooding made the soil rich and fertile, allowing plants to grow.

a stone carving of Hapi

Rivers continue to play a role in people's beliefs.

The River Ganges flows through India and Bangladesh.
It is **sacred** to Hindus. They believe that going into the
water washes away their problems.

Every 12 years, a festival called Kumbh Mela
(say: *kuhm may-lah*) is held. Around 70 million people
from India visit the Ganges over six weeks. They sing
holy songs and dip in the water.

Amazing rivers

This river in Colombia, South America, is known as the river of five colours. The colour is caused by a plant that grows in the riverbed. Visitors come to photograph it.

This river in Palawan, the Philippines, flows through a long cave system. Many people visit it to enjoy boat rides.

Caring for rivers

A river ecosystem is all the living and non-living things that exist in and around a river. Everything in an ecosystem is connected. For example, fish eat insects, and birds eat fish.

If something in the ecosystem changes, it can cause problems for animals and plants.

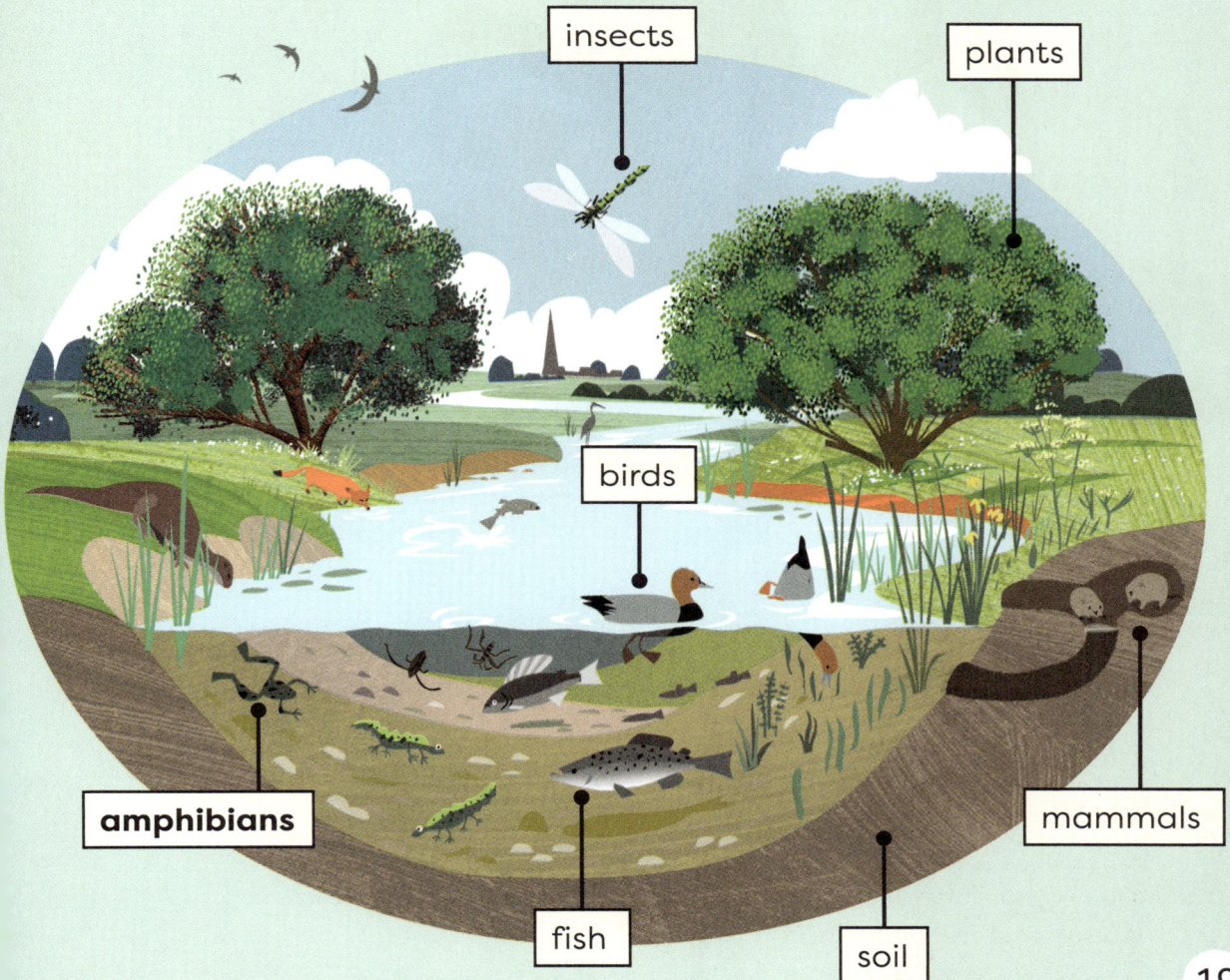

insects

plants

birds

amphibians

mammals

fish

soil

Scientists <u>monitor</u> rivers to make sure there is nothing bad in the water. They take <u>samples</u> to test for things like germs or chemicals.

A scientist taking a water <u>sample</u>.

By testing the water, they can make sure it stays safe for all the plants and animals that need it.

To <u>monitor</u> something is to watch it or test it regularly, in order to see what is happening.

A <u>sample</u> is a small amount that shows what something is like.

Unfortunately, humans are responsible for a lot of dangerous waste in rivers.

Factories and cars release pollution into the air. This can get into the water from rain.

Farmers use chemicals on their crops that can run into nearby rivers.

Animals can mistake plastic waste for food. They can also get tangled up in it.

To be responsible for something is to be the cause of it.

People are doing things to try and fix river pollution.

Some factories are using machines that create less pollution. People are encouraged to use their cars less often.

Farmers grow special plants along the edges of their fields. These plants soak up the chemicals so they do not run off into rivers.

You can help, too! Always recycle your litter.

By taking care of rivers, we can make sure they stay healthy so we can continue to <u>benefit</u> from them. Just like we have for thousands of years!

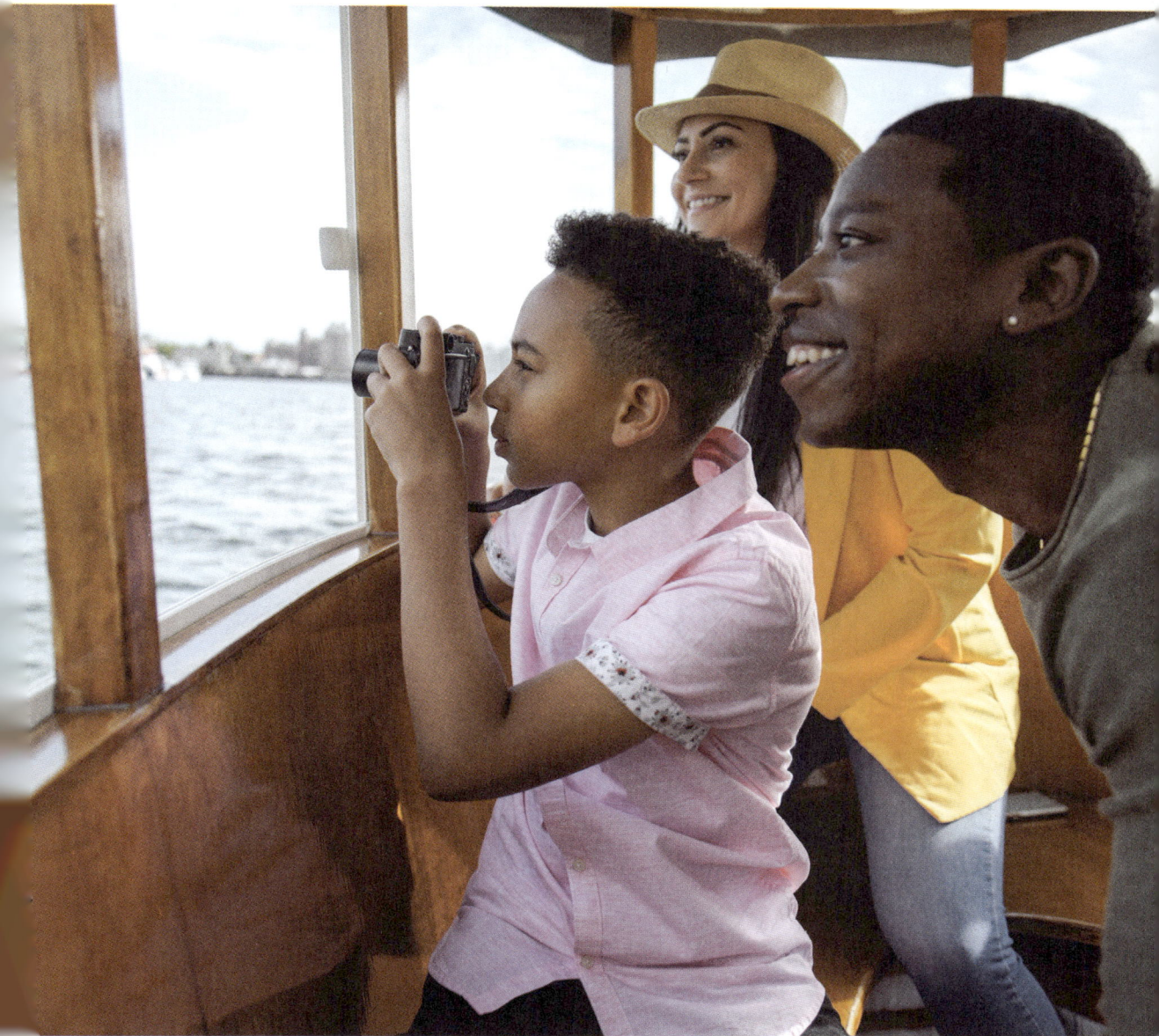

A <u>benefit</u> is something that is useful or helpful.

Glossary

amphibians: small animals that can live on land and also breathe under water

chemicals: substances used to help with particular things, like getting rid of germs or growing plants

civilizations: groups of people at particular times in history

cultures: the beliefs and behaviours of a group of people

dam: a barrier that holds back water

fertile: when soil contains everything it needs for plants to grow well

filters: equipment that removes unwanted things from a liquid

generator: a machine that turns energy into electricity

Indigenous peoples: people who have existed in a place since the earliest time

plant: a place with machinery to carry out a process

sacred: something with a religious meaning or purpose that is considered to be special

Index